international interiors

SHOWROOMS

John Beckmann

INTERIOR *details*

An Imprint of

P B C I N T E R N A T I O N A L, I N C.

Distributor to the book trade in the United States and Canada:

Rizzoli International Publications Inc.
300 Park Avenue South
New York, NY 10010

Distributor to the art trade in the United States and Canada:

PBC International, Inc.
One School Street
Glen Cove, NY 11542

Distributor throughout the rest of the world:

Hearst Books International
1350 Avenue of the Americas
New York, NY 10019

Library of Congress Cataloging-in-Publication Data

Beckmann, John.
    International interiors : showrooms   /   by John Beckmann.
            p.   cm. -- (Architecture & interior details)
    Includes index.
    ISBN 0-86636-196-0
    1. Showrooms--Decoration.   2. Interior decoration--History--20th
century.   3. Interior architecture--History--20th century.
I. Title. II. Series.
NK1980.B43   1993   92-41810
725'.21--dc20   CIP

CAVEAT—Information in this text is believed accurate, and will pose no
problem for the student or casual reader. However, the author was often
constrained by information contained in signed release forms, information
that could have been in error or not included at all. Any misinformation
(or lack of information) is the result of failure in these attestations.
The author has done whatever is possible to insure accuracy.

Cover separation, printing and binding by
Toppan Printing Co. [H.K.] Ltd. China

Typography by
TypeLink, Inc.

10 9 8 7 6 5 4 3 2 1

For Kyra and the angels in the architecture…

CONTENTS

FOREWORD

Thom Mayne   Morphosis *Santa Monica, California*

Architecture for interior spaces… interior spaces which share commerce as their *raison d'être*…the possibility of something other than a minus sum game from this scenario. A handful of works come to mind since the beginning of the modern movement which reveal a unity between art and life and which contain within them clear precursors of things to come. Van Doesburg's commission for the conversion of an eighteenth-century building designed by Francis Blondel, Cafe L'Aubette (Strasbourg, 1926–28), is one of these works.

Van Doesburg was especially attracted to the idea of life being integrated and unified with art…he understood an artist's task to be that of creating spiritual order in a chaotic world…the Newtonian world order based on gravity was superseded in his works by an architecture which seemed to hover in space and time. Many of the issues in the relationship between art and architecture upon which Van Doesburg focused his energy remain with us and are again under consideration today. His interests were to shape the environment into an artistic whole, to liberate mankind from the mundane, and to exert a moral effect. His strategies produced an open architecture, undermining a building's stability through color and light and through the use of contrasts and dissonances. It is with the project for L'Aubette that Van Doesburg found his opportunity to place man *within* the painting; architecture and painting were thus partnered to produce the expression of a unitary, tangible object.

And so it is this relatively non-prolific painter/architect/writer/philosopher who comes to mind for me when I ruminate on the potential for integrity and meaning in commercial, interior architecture. A man who produced little, but who provided (through his rigor) an illumination for that which would follow. The work here, like that of Van Doesburg's L'Aubette, utilizes the commercial circumstance to pursue a larger idea or concept. There is a thread running through these projects through which one can trace a resistance to the strictures of program and rule. It is through this resistance that L'Aubette was produced, that all meaningful work is produced…these works are about a process of discovering one's own beliefs and values and aspiring to pursue (or advance) new questions regarding the relevancies of our time.

INTRODUCTION

John Beckmann

As we approach the end of an extraordinarily rich and complex century, can any apparent changes be seen in the maelstrom of current architectural and design discourse? Clearly, no *Fin de Siècle* has emerged—at least it has not reared its ugly head as of this writing. What is clear, however, is that we have entered into a period of critical silence and contemplation. The initial purity of the Modern Movement has lost its youthful innocence, and now Modernism is merely a superficial image of its original utopian tenets. Its opposite parody, Post Modernism, has left us with nothing more than a handful of ambiguous buildings which announce their own superficiality.

The substantial, homogeneous concepts of space derived from classical Greek geometry have given way to a fractured, discontinuous and disruptive view of representation. The former codifications established by our architectural heritage—unity, symmetry, orthography—have been permanently altered by architects and designers like Frank Gehry, Coop Himmelblau, Daniel Libeskind, Rem Koolhaas, Ettore Sottsass, Alessandro Mendini and many others. This disintegration of fixed positions has led to individual and, hence, more subjective approaches, thus fostering a rather delirious turnover of architectural fashions and takes. The new design is not engaging a style or a methodology but, on the contrary, is seeking a way to represent an increasingly accelerated, heterogeneous and digitized world view. What we are witnessing is the progressive emergence of form-images which are analogous to the instantaneous, unstable and fleeting luminous emissions that flicker from our television screens and computer monitors—ultimately resulting in a reception rather than a perception.

Design is at times a painstaking, merciless and unforgiving field of endeavor, its practitioners and their clients forever condemned to live with their mistakes. The younger generation of professionals is beginning to reject the values on which existing design has been based. They seek, instead, to liberate space, much as the avant-garde writers of previous generations sought to free their pages from plot/structures and narratives. Concepts like function, program and order are being brushed aside in favor of more open, expressive, emotional and sometimes even lyrical gestures. This new generation seems confident that design is undergoing a great, almost psychic manifestation, and with this a leap in consciousness will most inevitably follow.

This non-hierarchical, destratified and freewheeling tendency can be seen in a number of projects shown in this book, notably Cordero Progetti's work for C.P. Company, Massimo Morozzi's projects for Edra, and Ron Arad's One Off showroom in London.

Constructivist in approach, C.P. Company's flagship showroom/retail space, in Manhattan's historic, wedge-shaped Flatiron Building, presents us with a sphinx-like riddle. Certainly, to the casual Saturday shopper, the enigmatic nature of a shop whose interior is concealed behind highway guard-rails must, at first glance, seem rather strange.

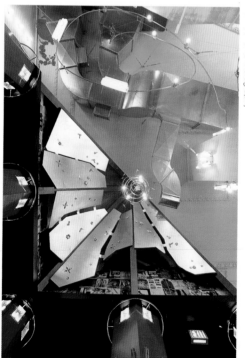

Whirling guard-rails (which serve as the clothing display system) have been grafted onto the walls in a feverish display of architectural gymnastics. Industrial fluorescent lighting fixtures are wrapped in spiraling chromed bars, draped in chain mail fabric and dangling crystals, haphazardly suspended from the ceiling. In a world where symbols have become merchandise, the architects have reacted by literally sticking the urban context blatantly "in our faces," thereby impeding our first reading. Combining child-like naivete with Italian bravura, Cordero Progetti have chosen to discard some of fashion retailing's most sacrosanct rules and in doing so have created a project infused with a fiendish grace.

In the evocative Mediterranean light of Sardinia, Massimo Morozzi & Company have created a storybook of "synthetic" sitting-rooms to display Edra's line of upholstered seating. Morozzi's spaces are "telematic" narratives designed to tell "Room Tales" about heightened comforts and moods. Each room or tale has a theme, Morozzi states, "like the beads of a polychrome necklace; romantic and sugary like just-blossomed young girls, haughty like ladies of a good family, mysterious and dark, as though they were the scenery of a spy story, surrealistic like some of Breton's pictures, gaudy like the images of America's 'on the road movies.'"

Giacomo Giannini

The French theoretician of communication Paul Virilio believes "The most insidious un-information is caused by the saturation of the information of too many images similar to each other, too many already said things, asphyxia of real or fake values." Imbued with Virilio's post-structuralist ideas as well as previous revelations from Italian neo-radical groups such as Memphis and Alchimia, Morozzi's "fake settings" speak

to us from a metalinguistic vantage point, visually reinterpreted in a "Moldovaresque" manner and repackaged for an image-bombarded, over-stimulated MTV generation. Indeed, they are laughing at us, as we laugh back.

Ron Arad's "eccentric" new furniture showroom and design offices in northwest London rise from a derelict courtyard like a phoenix from its ashes. From under a winged roof form of expanded metal, a shell structure of PVC plastic and "calligraphic columns" serves as a physical metaphor for the studio's creative process.

The lightweight, translucent roof membrane grew out of a search for a material relatively quick to build with and easy to use. The shape of the roof is derived from the structural principle of a tensioned membrane, restrained by the curvature and compressive forces of the expanded metal shell.

Christof Kircherer

The interior conception is a tour de force and a logical leap from Arad's previous experiments in defiantly sculptural furniture. Here the floor is treated as a three-dimensional surface; its undulating form creates a soft transition between the showroom and design office. Steel "calligraphic columns" serve as a radial track for rotating windows, creating a flexible "soft window" (made from 8mm-thick industrial PVC), which can be opened

and fixed into any position. An arched steel bridge or ramp vaults from the "hill" to the mezzanine level, which was constructed as a hollow box section to conceal the HVAC ducts, at the same time serving as an inventive display area.

In totality and scope, One Off's new digs represent Ron Arad's most ambitious and triumphant project to date, further solidifying his reputation as a unique inventor of bold forms and clever manipulator of materials.

As the aforementioned projects and the other fine works featured in this book indicate, the previous "isms" of recent years are favorably being dismantled and reformulated by a generation of independent thinkers, not simply as roads to a goal, but through the undertaking of processes more akin to a magician trafficking the unknown. Their efforts, independent of prosthetic devices and stylistic cliches, will provide conduits of thought for the generation, projection and transmutation of new vessels for the senses.

Author's Note

For organization's sake, I've chosen to arrange the contents/projects herein under loosely defined chapter headings—Constructivist, Rationalist, Eccentric, Synthetic and Corporate, respectively. Let it be understood that my intention for doing so is not simply to tag a stylistic label on a project, but to reflect and clarify for the general reader the various multivalent representational tendencies, positions or tactics that are currently prevalent among the varied discourse of architecture and design, so that comparisons can be made between projects that share a similar intention of expression or purpose.

Although this book focuses on showrooms, a certain "gray" area nevertheless does exist. With the high price of commercial real-estate, more and more companies are being forced to consolidate their retailing and wholesale operations. This trend is particularly evident in Europe and will undoubtedly continue in the future. I've taken the liberty of including a few dual projects in the belief that their worth will prove relevant to anyone consulting this book for future reference.

The Value of Nothing

Ross Anderson   Anderson/Schwartz Architects *New York, New York*

The generic program usually assigned to showrooms and studios acknowledges the role of architecture as something other than the accommodation of program and the provision of comfort. By shaping pragmatic concerns into dense configurations, a spatial looseness remains that allows for a kind of "otherness." It is in this "otherness" where intention, emotion, affirmation, tactility and ritualistic display coexist.

In *haiku* poetry, eloquent silence, concealment, and spare use of words suggest a fully rendered, total experience. A *Noh* play conveys meaning through silence to the most striking and significant passages, just as calligraphy requires a collaboration between line and empty space. When a component of emptiness is provided in a showroom, displayed objects (articles of fashion) condense; that is, they find their own contrast and stand out in relief. These objects become participants in the changing, configural quality of place where solitude also has exhibition value. This creates a place where spontaneous, unstructured immersion is possible.

While the business component of the enterprise remains concealed, there is a sense that some of what is being produced

has been captured or detained for viewing. The Japanese art of arranging plants and flowers in water—*Ikebana*—suggests that these captured elements energize and activate a modern space. Their presence modifies, manipulates, enhances, focuses and helps shape space. A form of consecration occurs. The display of fashion, whether on a model moving in space, or arranged on a table or shelf, accomplishes this same consecration.

Our intentions have been to provide a contemplative, ritualistic approach to the object. To suggest an abstracted landscape within, or perhaps capture a borrowed view. To be modern as well as return to more primal sources. To have a collective experience as well as a solitary one. To give substance to the spectacle of glamour…a place where distraction becomes intoxication.

Between Process and Product

Terry Dwan   Studio Citterio Dwan *Milan, Italy*

The ambiguous point lying within the combined fields of architecture/industrial design can require a delicate relationship with both the patronage and the industry, as specifically seen in showroom design.

While I am an architect, and my partner Antonio Citterio is an architect and industrial designer, we have worked together for the past seven years, exchanging experiences derived from these diverse activities. The most frequently asked question deals with the interface between the two, and it is difficult to clearly distinguish the points uniting and dividing these roles.

Historically, industrial design was considered a decorative art and therefore seemed less encumbered by pragmatic considerations. Due to growing specialization in industry in North America, industrial designers have often lacked training in the field of architecture and vice versa. Architectural offices are generally separate from those of industrial designers, whereas in Italy, where we practice, and other European countries the two are united.

In the context of the European tradition, an architect was trained in many of the arts, methodologically and ideologically. Education has maintained this cultural basis while often eliminating the pragmatic and tactile. Modernity, also with its supposition of ideas, both literate and repeatable, has abstracted certain intuitions rendering them useless in what would otherwise be profound ritual objects.

In these past years the cult of images has surpassed the cultivation of ideas, obeying the laws of the marketplace of information. The result is the increased frequency of novelties. Magazines by now monopolize industrial design asking continually for new projects to publish and creating a mechanism of "over production." Each year we see the creation of thousands of prototypes of which only 2 percent are actually realized. The majority of these objects are created only for their shock value. This proliferation of items has degenerated the concept of the collective memory, from which many objects were born, and expresses both the refusal of the modern as well as the failure therein.

We therefore recognize in confronting the designing of showroom space, that the products for which the space is destined, as actors on a stage, are protagonists. Therein lies a relationship of reciprocal stim-

ulation between the product and the space. We often take mechanically produced objects and try to render them spontaneous through a juxtaposition with a space produced in an artisanly manner. In our projects we use materials considered neither high-tech nor noble such as brick, concrete stucco, zinc, copper, and steel, without altering their origi-

nal nature. These become elements in a well-defined language, where only the absolutely necessary survives.

For example, with furniture design products, their image is often spontaneous, lyrical and colorful, as in the case of the products displayed in the Obayashi "Corrente" showroom in Tokyo. They are manufactured, however, in a rigorously systematic and mechanical manner, with the high volume and huge capital investments common to all industrial processes.

The resulting tension comes from the highly artisan architecture, whose image is ironically rendered as rigorous, mechanical and privy of any ornament. Circulation elements are a recurring consideration for the organization of the display spaces, and have determined the key points of a specific language for stairs, ramps and catwalks.

Our relationship with the client is also essential to the realization of the project. While we are concerned with creating the appropriate display space for the product at hand it also becomes necessary to follow the client's philosophy which is apt to change as the years pass.

At the turn of the century the conditions of growth and industrial progress produced a number of affluent art patrons who worked directly with artists and architects to realize their ideological dreams. This clientele decisively influenced the arts as a group. Today economic tendencies differ, but the importance of their influence has not changed.

We have had the fortune to meet three "personality" clients: Piero Busnelli for B&B furniture company, Doug Tompkins for Esprit de Corps fashion company, and Rolf and Raymond Feldbaum for Vitra. For all three we have produced objects, various interior exhibition space, as well as architecture. In the case of Vitra and B&B, the product preceded their respective showrooms, while the reverse was true for Esprit de Corps. Despite these differences, the client has remained a pivotal force.

Design/Commerce Strategies

Henry Smith-Miller Smith-Miller + Hawkinson *New York, New York*

The commodification of architectural design in contemporary society presents a peculiar paradox in the case of the showroom. On the one hand, architecture and design are commonly presumed to function in the service of society, which can be understood as maintaining the "status quo," representing and bolstering the already known, proven and acceptable, as in the "classic," blue Tiffany gift box.

On the other hand, invention and innovation are also common characteristics of the architectural design product, signifying change and the "new." When marketing "new," the role of invention and innovation and the normative role of design "in the service of" are in conflict.

In many showrooms, design is often equated with the object being "sold." This motivated alliance and the typical machinations of a consumer market which result in the rapid obsolescence of the design product, creates a need for constant revision of not only the product being sold but also its context.

Alignment of motive is a vehicle for the space of commodity. But so is its opposite, the disjunctive presentation. In the first case, that of alignment, i.e., the seamlessness of the Ralph Lauren "Polo Lounge" and its products, the sale object may be difficult to differentiate from the setting. In the disjunc-

tive format, the very difference in setting foregrounds the object and highlights its newness.

Neither of these strategies can be said to be critical of the circular production of new goods and of desire for these goods.

A third format allows for critical representation and acknowledgment of the motives of commodification, even while accommodating the goods. In the case of

Toshiko Mori's initial designs for the New York based "Comme des Garçons" shop in Bendel's, as well as the later "Shirt Shop" on West Broadway in SoHo, the deliberate effacement of the product being sold in the showroom presented an "image" which challenged the normative role of design in the service of the market.

The program of commerce which is a given in the conceptualization of any showroom can be seen as a challenge to examine the role of design in society. Aligned with, in the service of, or sometimes critical of the agenda of commerce, the showroom represents a highly visible microcosm of the role of architecture in society, a paradigm for the study of contemporary attitudes and ideas.

Japanese Design in the '90s

Shigeru Uchida   Studio 80   *Tokyo, Japan*

Interior design in Japan is unique in that it developed to a large degree within the domain of commercial spaces as opposed to most countries in which it developed within residential spaces. This can be attributed to the widespread changes that have occurred within Japanese society since the 1970s. The

Koichi Inakoshi

Japanese economy has flourished since that time, and this has been reflected in unprecedented expansion in all areas of the business world. It is this expansion that has given Japanese designers the freedom to experiment and to establish a unique character with which to influence the life-style of a new era.

Competition has had both positive and negative effects on Japanese interior design. The desire of manufacturers and retailers to differentiate their products has spurred designers to become more creative in their work, yet at the same time it has resulted in a loss of control, and reduced interior design to simply a tool for sales promotion.

The '90s in Japan is therefore a crucial decade. Facing a calm era following the rampant growth and expansion of the '80s, it is our task to bring some measure of control back into the design process. By taking into account family and community standards, social order, and both the regional and global environment, we must design in a manner which both reduces waste and fosters social responsibility.

The Showroom as Theater

Masanori Umeda U-MetaDesign, Inc. *Tokyo, Japan*

The role of designers in today's highly information-oriented society is not only to design functions or forms of products or space in the process of corporate business. Designers are now requested to be the incarnators of their clients' developing power, while making the most of the operational resources of those clients. It is necessary for them to create an explicit, unique and specific concept for each company and to supply design works conveying clear messages. A showroom is an important space for a company to realize its corporate identity.

It is both a high-touch and real-time space which stimulates people's senses. It also can be said to be the face of the company, or space with a drama. The drama can include various roles like main and sub-characters and even a clown; products could be the main character at one time, and space or human beings at another. Various kinds of dramas are performed, in which space and products talk to people and make them smile, surprised and pleased. One might say that designers are similar to writers or directors of dramas.

"The train had passed through the long tunnel on the border and the snow country spread out there." To design a space always reminds me of this first sentence of the famous novel *Yukiguni (Snow Country)* by Yasunari Kawabata. As the quotation illustrates, the most important theme to me is how strongly my design works can appeal to people's senses and emotions, and it is needless to say that the works should have great originality and historical value.

My design concept is "meta design." The method is sometimes expressed metaphysically, and for some objects, metabolically or metaphorically. At the same time, however, "meta" means "half" in Italian. Therefore I'm always in agony, struggling to create products and space that go beyond design concepts in the past. Possibly my design works are like ephemeral flowers which silently bloom in the valley between going and coming generations in the end of the century.

con · struc · tiv · ist *adj* anti-teleological, non-hierarchical, polyvalent space.

C. P. COMPANY

PRODUCT: Men's clothing
New York, NY

C.P. Company is situated on the ground floor of the world-famous Flatiron Building on Manhattan's lower Fifth Avenue. Here Turinese architects Toni Cordero and Joann Paul have employed neo-futurist techniques, infusing the interior with an energy Giacomo Balla or Marinetti would have been proud of. Every well-worn fashion merchandising technique has been visibly dismantled, in an effort to express the dynamic sensations of an accelerated city.

As Marinetti states in the first Futurist manifesto of 1909: "Except in struggle there is no more beauty. No work without an aggressive character can be a masterpiece. Poetry must be conceived as a violent attack on the unknown forces…. " At C.P. Company, spiraling highway guard rails (which function as the clothing display racks) whirl dervish-like around the interior volume, covering up the shop windows in the process. Ad-hoc industrial lighting fixtures, wrapped in chain mail fabric, bent chrome wires and crystals torn off of old-fashioned chandeliers combine to create an environment of ordered chaos, at once fractured and poetic.

CLIENT: **C.P. Company** PRODUCT: **Men's clothing** DESIGNERS: **Toni Cordero and Joann Paul** PHOTOGRAPHY: **Tom Schierlitz Photography**

Tom Schierlitz Photography

Tom Schierlitz Photography

Tom Schierlitz Photography

FINAL IMAGE

PRODUCT: Digital imaging
New York, NY

Final Image, designed by Uvegi Associates, is a digital imaging showroom/retail shop located on Manhattan's Upper West Side. The designers' brief was to accommodate a customer servicing area, provide facilities for a Kodak "create-a-print" developing machine, an in-house digital imaging area (visible to the public), as well as providing for a user-friendly, "state-of-the-art" interactive environment to highlight the new photo CD technology equipment and gamewares.

Faced with a complicated brief, equipment requirements and a mere 600 square feet of usable space, Uvegi Associates set about initiating a series of bold spatial manipulations.

The initial conceptual act of rotating and skewing the green glass facade anticipates and defines a strong visible diagonal which predominates into the interior. A propped, cantilevered stainless steel handrail system supports the freestanding wall of green glass panels and defines the raised "image-plex" work area. This glass membrane is bisected by a 10-foot-high, perforated, anodized aluminum cylinder (silo) which encloses the "create-a-print" machine, providing customers with a hands-on color developing center, where prints from negatives can be had in four minutes.

Further inventions include the rolling storage systems, which glide along a wall in recessed tracks, facilitating order processing. The wall directly opposite is sloped 10 degrees and is clad in a 2-foot-by-2-foot maple plywood grid, which accommodates video monitors and interactive photo CD players. A gracefully arched ceiling canopy adds a sensual touch to the strictly tectonic exercises.

Throughout, the project remains a sensitive work, counterpoising hightech machines with sculptural forms in a warm, natural environment where a great deal of attention was paid to detailing.

CLIENT: **Final Image** PRODUCT: **Digital imaging** DESIGN FIRM: **Uvegi Associates, Inc.** PRINCIPAL IN CHARGE: **Harry Uvegi** PROJECT DESIGNERS: **Harry Uvegi and John Beckmann** DESIGN TEAM: **Harry Uvegi, John Beckmann, Ron Walker** PHOTOGRAPHY: **Jeff Vaughan**

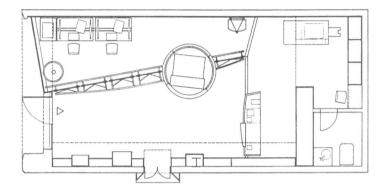

Jeff Vaughan

Jeff Vaughan

MAP

PRODUCT: Contemporary funiture
Melbourne, Australia

The MAP showroom, designed by Chris Connell to display his own research into furniture, integrates a severe minimal aesthetic with a dynamic approach to architectural composition. Working within the confines of a modest budget, Connell's intent throughout this project was to achieve the maximum amount of usable space and flexibility. Leaving the architectural envelope intact, Connell designed a series of angled and sloping colored-plaster walls, behind which are an office and storage zones. The only other element designed for the space is a movable aluminum beam, which functions as a sales-counter and a display platform. MAP displays only two or three designs at any one given time.

CLIENT: **Christopher Connell**   PRODUCT: **Contemporary furniture**   DESIGNER: **Christopher Connell**   PHOTOGRAPHY: © **Trevor Mein Photography**

ISAAC MIZRAHI
PRODUCT: Women's and men's clothing
New York, NY

Isaac Mizrahi's studio, showroom and offices comprise two floors of a turn-of-the-century industrial loft building in SoHo, totaling some 12,000 square feet. The architects' programmatic brief was to design a neutral background, while providing offices for 20 employees, showrooms, runways accommodating fashion shows, design studios and fitting rooms.

The architects inserted a plywood and poplar wall or "slot" which separates display and studio areas from semi-enclosed offices and conference rooms contained within. The "slot" with its rhythmic openings serves as a theatrical backdrop for the seasonal fashion activities, yet allows for the existing duct work and piping to penetrate and co-exist. To further distinguish between public and private areas, Anderson specified runway/corridors of high-gloss white epoxy floors.

On the fourth floor, a mysterious, skewed, maple-veneer box trimmed in raw steel angles serves as the fitting room. A large, pivoting curved wood door infilled with fiberglass-impregnated paper provides entry into the inner sanctum. Here, as is evident throughout, discerning attention was paid to elevating common materials, establishing a discrete palette of colors and constructing a concise architectural envelope, to create a calm and sophisticated environment.

CLIENT: **Isaac Mizrahi and Company** PRODUCT: **Women's and men's clothing**
ARCHITECTS: **Anderson/Schwartz Architects** PARTNER IN CHARGE:
Ross Anderson PROJECT ARCHITECT: **M.J. Sagan** PROJECT TEAM:
Joanne M. Robinson, Caroline A.A. Schiele, Frederic Schwartz, Samuel Tonos, Janice Kitchen, Eric Robbins PHOTOGRAPHY:
© **Michael Moran**

RAPID INDUSTRIAL PLASTICS

PRODUCT: Industrial plastics
Jersey City, NJ

Jersey City is not known for its innovative architecture and is certainly not to be found in any guidebooks on the subject. In fact, the outskirts of Jersey City are primarily full of factories and other manufacturing facilities. Amidst this industrial hubris is Donna Selene Seftel's addition to Rapid Industrial Plastics.

The extension to the '60s pancake office building and factory required new offices for salespeople, two offices for the partners, a showroom and sample room. Both partners requested a view from the front of the building where the Statue of Liberty and World Trade Center are in clear sight. They also requested a highly visible sign, noticeable from the nearby New Jersey Turnpike.

Ms. Seftel's conceptual floor plan was inspired "by the profiles of buildings as they appear when one stands at the intersection of two city streets and looks up into the sky. The basic cross seen at the ground plane undergoes a series of transformations according to the various heights and setbacks of the corner blocks." This masonry building is thus notched, cut, pierced and generally inscribed according to a high level of architectural compositioning methods, which reveal the very nature of a "plastic intelligence" at work.

Custom-designed furniture was created for the offices and showrooms using the same rigorous methods. All plastic samples are hidden from view, to keep the work surfaces free from distractions.

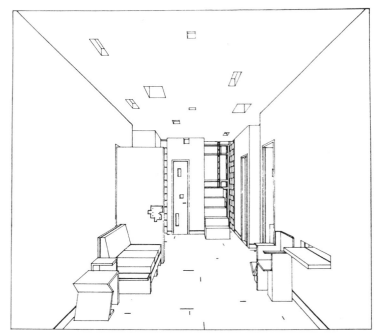

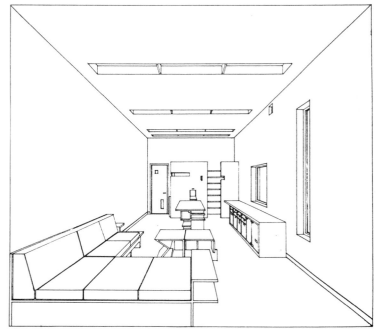

CLIENT: **Rapid Industrial Plastics**   PRODUCT: **Industrial plastics**   DESIGNER:
Donna Selene Seftel Architects   PRINCIPAL IN CHARGE: **Donna Selene Seftel**
PHOTOGRAPHY: © **Eduard Hueber-Arch Photo; Donna Selene Seftel**

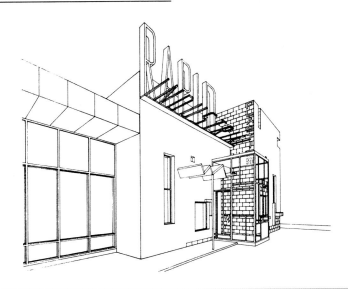

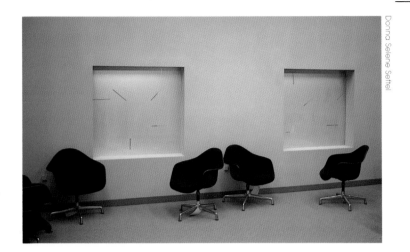

REACH NETWORKS

PRODUCT: Software
New York, NY

Reach Networks, Inc., a progressive software company housed in an industrial loft in the SoHo section of Manhattan, requested offices that were private, yet conveyed a sense of openness to newer ways of communication and information management. Anderson/Schwartz dealt with the programmatic requirements by creating a series of gyrated walls, screens and cabinets.

A "room without walls," defined by a raised concrete tile platform centered within the four existing columns, acts as the product display area. A video monitor which spans the width of the office displays the "Product." Chairs for this area were designed to convey the informality of the company.

The plaster wall attached to the face of the office modules is perforated with small horizontal and vertical slots that allow visual contact and light penetration. The wall is a composed image of light and shadow, solid and void, that is reminiscent of computer cards of recent history.

The conference area is behind a plywood cabinet that is smoke-finished with hand-applied graphite. A 16-foot-long conference table of cherry and glass extends through the window into the view beyond.

© Michael Moran

CLIENT: **Reach Networks, Inc.** PRODUCT: **Software** ARCHITECTS: **Anderson/Schwartz Architects** PARTNER IN CHARGE: **Ross Anderson** PROJECT ARCHITECT: **M.J. Sagan** PROJECT TEAM: **Joanne M. Robinson, Caroline A.A. Schiele** PHOTOGRAPHY: © **Michael Moran**

© Michael Moran

© Michael Moran

LEON MAX

PRODUCT: Women's contemporary clothing
Los Angeles, CA

The conversion of a former industrial space to a clothing showroom provided Morphosis with a unique laboratory to explore the architectural process.

A wrapper, or liner, made up of movable modular storage units, fabricated with perforated metal surfaces, was created inside the perimeter walls to provide for merchandise storage. It also allows the space behind to be used for private offices. This new container reinforces the existing spatial boundaries and provides a visual backdrop for the four freestanding Morphosis-designed machines.

These machines/objects were designed to accommodate reception, runway, conference room and reception areas. Beyond making reference to the spatial and dynamic aspects of architecture, they affirm the presence of an artistic intervention, engaging in a dialogue within the warehouse topology. Of particular interest are the sliding partitions which are clad in plywood and set into steel frames which rotate on a large, hinged mechanical armature.

CLIENT: **Leon Max** PRODUCT: **Women's contemporary clothing** DESIGN FIRM:
Morphosis PRINCIPALS IN CHARGE: **Thom Mayne and Michael Rotondi**
PROJECT ARCHITECTS: **Kiyokazu Arai and Will Sharp** DESIGN TEAM:
Stephanie Adolf, Craig Burdick, Andrea Claire, Christoper Oakley
PHOTOGRAPHY: © **Farshid Assassi/Assassi Productions**

ra·tio·nal·ist *adj* abstraction based upon reason; formal and purist.

CONCORD LIGHTING

PRODUCT: Lighting
London, England

Julian Powell-Tuck and Associates Ltd. have created a dramatic and functional laboratory for product display/demonstration and offices for Concord Lighting. As a design consultant to Concord over the past eight years, Powell-Tuck had been responsible for the company's successful "Optics" and "Myriad" low voltage range of products.

Concord chose the ground, mezzanine and basement areas of an early seventies office block in High Holborn as their site. Due to budgetary restrictions, the company opted to allocate the better part of their budget to the showroom area proper, leaving the existing facade and mezzanine areas intact. Powell-Tuck's design solution separated the showroom into three areas, layering back from the glass facade.

The first and most public area is a tall dramatic space that serves to launch new products and demonstrate lighting within an architectural space. It can also function as a venue to host lighting events. Here, and in the adjoining reception area, Concord Lighting products can be seen in a typical environment in which they might be used.

The next layer is seen as a three-dimensional catalogue of lighting products. It is a user-friendly area where visitors can discuss particular requirements. Large white hinged or sliding screens provide privacy, block and control daylight and provide a surface on which to demonstrate lighting.

The final layer, a "backstage" area, accommodates a line of small offices, with each office providing various lighting demonstration zones.

White painted walls, maple flooring and gray carpets throughout provide a neutral background so as not to distract from the lighting products or colors.

© John Edward Linden Inset: © John Edward Linden

CLIENT: **GTE Concord Lighting Ltd.** PRODUCT: **Lighting** DESIGN FIRM: **Powell-Tuck Associates Ltd.** DESIGNER: **Julian Powell-Tuck** DESIGN TEAM: **Angus Shepherd, Peter Murray, Krishna Money, Adrian Lees** PHOTOGRAPHY: **© John Edward Linden**

THE INSIDE ED

© John Edward Linden

© John Edward Linden

© John Edward Linden

© John Edward Linden

NICOLE FARHI
PRODUCT: Women's and men's clothing
London, England

Briefed to create a timeless interior for Nicole Farhi's wholesale showroom, Din Associates installed a glass atrium over a spacious show area. The scheme takes its inspiration from nineteenth-century conservatories, railway stations and arcades.

The showroom is entered through two clear glass-paneled doors in a 12-foot-high timber screen fixed to the cross beam under the first truss of the roof light. Diffused glass is used for the remaining panels.

In the reception area, a blue sofa is combined with a custom-made American oak table and desk with distinctive green paneling. Farhi's first men's collection is displayed separately in a room dominated by Matthew Hilton's huge mirror and wooden table.

The walls and timber are the color of raw silk, with wrought iron columns and the roof light structures painted a fresh mint green, all combining to evoke a cafe-like atmosphere.

CLIENT: **Nicole Farhi** PRODUCT: **Women's and men's clothing** DESIGNER: **Din Associates Ltd.** DESIGN DIRECTOR: **John Harvey** DESIGN ASSOCIATE: **Lesley Batchelor** PHOTOGRAPHY: **Peter Cook**

Peter Cook

Peter Cook

IB OFFICE
PRODUCT: Contract furniture
Padua, Italy

On the ground floor of a building flanked by the Bacchiglione canal on one side, and by an historic ancient Roman passageway on the other, Umberto Riva and associates have created a work of spartan beauty. The design is based on a multiplication of viewpoints, perceptual ambiguities and a certain casual formal arrangement. Ultimately, however, the project is composed of a sensitive manipulation of modulated light, both natural and artificial.

Riva's design is essentially confined to the perimeter envelope, the window wall along the bypass; the opposite wall (which is part of the Roman wall); the glazed obliquely shaped vestibule; the end wall; the ceiling and the polished concrete floor.

The existing windows along the street side are screened by a series of paired, pivoting, sand-etched panels, which are fastened to Istria stone plinth bases. An artificial light source has been placed behind one of these panels, allowing it to act as a diffuser, producing a mobile light system of great resonance.

Along the wall directly opposite, a single small porthole aperture is perceptively doubled by a mirror recessed into the corner of an angled wall. An additional light source, identical to the previous ones described, is housed vertically creating a deliberate distortion by reflecting varying cuts of different depths and shapes.

At the rear of the showroom, in front of an ochre-colored wall, a suspended arm-lamp pierces through a large porthole window. It projects out into the space, acting as a direct visual counterpoint to an identical fixture placed in the front vestibule. The other constructed element is a wedge-shaped wall panelled in Okume wood, which has been treated with white lead and perforated by openings/niches, one of which leads to a staircase.

Riva's work, here expressed through his unified handling of details and light, achieves an architecture saturated with the utmost clarity.

CLIENT: **IB Office** PRODUCT: **Contract furniture** DESIGNERS: **Umberto Riva, Architect, with Francesca Riva, Giacomo Borella, Alberto Fanton, Paola Froncillo** PHOTOGRAPHY: **Francesco Radino**

SCOTT HOWARD BUILDING
PRODUCT: Contract furniture
London, England

Allies and Morrison were commissioned by Scott Howard (agents for the Haller office system) to design their new showroom on the site of St. James Church, constructed in 1787. The church was damaged by a bomb in World War I and remodeled in the 1930s before it was deemed structurally unsound and demolished in 1983. The demolition was approved by the local building authorities and the church commissioners, who gave permission for office use on the site "provided that the new building would follow in replica the form of the original structure."

An office building clearly bears no relation to a church. After much debate, two distinct features of the earlier building were identified as being of prime importance, the first being the original stucco facade, the second the simple massing of the building within the landscape setting of the courtyard, which survives today as a public park.

Faced with a daunting task, Allies and Morrison set about developing a dialogue with the church facade and massing, with the common concerns of creating a good, well-lit, functional office space.

The architects have thoughtfully composed a building within a building, with subtle notations and traces being expressed in varying rhythmic grids along its exterior skin.

The interior galleries are quiet and sedate, and a great deal of attention was paid to the detailing of the rich language of the entrance bridge balustrade.

CLIENT: **Scott Howard Properties Ltd.** PRODUCT: **Contract furniture** ARCHITECTS: **Allies and Morrison** PROJECT ARCHITECTS: **Bob Allies, Graham Morrison, Joanna Green** PHOTOGRAPHY: **Peter Cook**

Peter Cook Inset: Peter Cook

VITRA-FRANCE

Vitra's new Paris showroom, designed by Antonio Citterio and Terry Dwan, occupies three floors of showrooms, exhibition spaces and offices, in a building within walking distance from the Seine, the Eiffel Tower and Montparnasse. The building is characterized by its square courtyard and extraordinary glass skylight.

Citterio/Dwan's approach to the design of this project was to exploit the existing architecture to its fullest. Small rooms are articulated by thick wall openings on axis with the entry, which is square, and defined by a structure of studded columns and exposed steel beams. The addition of a new metal staircase creates a separation between the two areas.

At the end of the hall one can catch a glimpse of the three levels of the interior court; the showroom space and its wall toward the gallery/hall provides a real facade that opens toward the interior.

Characterized by extreme spareness of materials and colors, the space functions more as an art gallery. The architects believe that Vitra's furniture, which embodies form united with technology, requires no further embellishment.

Gabriele Basilico

Gabriele Basilico

SHOWROOM: **Vitra** PRODUCT: **Contract furniture** DESIGN FIRM: **Studio Citterio Dwan** PARTNERS IN CHARGE: **Antonio Citterio and Terry Dwan, with Patricia Viel** PHOTOGRAPHY: **Gabriele Basilico**

Gabriele Basilico

PETER JOSEPH
PRODUCT: Furniture and art
New York, NY

The Peter Joseph Gallery exhibits some of the finest examples of furniture and objects designed by artists and architects, particularly those living and working in the United States. The inaugural exhibition was dedicated to the works of the well-known artist/cabinetmaker Wendell Castle.

The gallery is housed in some 6,000 square feet of prime real estate on Manhattan's Fifth Avenue and 57th Street. The architect's brief was to accommodate a reception gallery, main and secondary galleries, as well as private offices for the director and staff.

Peter J. Zweig's efforts are apparent upon entering the round, dramatically spot-lit reception gallery, where a single object is usually displayed. The main gallery and the various secondary galleries have all been laid out in accordance with the existing ceiling structural grid. Pale maple flooring was used throughout, along with some very subtle detailing, which included the flush baseboard reveals and coffered light slots in the ceiling, thus avoiding the usual pitfalls of unsightly distractions.

The design contributes an understated elegance suitable for the display of art and furniture of a high caliber.

CLIENT: **Peter Joseph Gallery** PRODUCT: **Furniture and art** DESIGNER:
Peter Jay Zweig, FAIA PHOTOGRAPHY: **Michael Galatis**

Michael Galatis

Michael Galatis

Michael Galatis

CARMEN FURNITURE

PRODUCT: Contract furniture *Sydney, Australia*

The new showroom for Carmen Furniture is housed in a 2,750-square-foot, one-hundred-year-old loft-type building formerly used for wool storage. Burley Katon Halliday's brief required that the space be overhauled to include a showroom, reception area and office zones.

Iain Halliday and his design team initiated a meticulous restoration of the existing space, retaining many of its positive qualities such as the exposed wood ceiling joists. The striking entry staircase leads up to the reception area which, with its 20-foot-long banquette and round porthole windows, is reminiscent of some lavish luxury ocean liner.

In the main showroom, the elegant cross-shaped metal columns, terrazzo flooring, translucent lighting baffles and atmospheric scrim laid across the window all combine to create an austere, yet highly physical setting.

Sharrin Rees Photography

Sharrin Rees Photography

CLIENT: **Carmen Furniture** PRODUCT: **Contract furniture** DESIGN FIRM:
Burley Katon Halliday PARTNER IN CHARGE: **Iain Halliday** DESIGN TEAM:
Iain Halliday, Tim Allison, David Seldon, Sue Melosu PHOTOGRAPHY:
Sharrin Rees Photography

Sharrin Rees Photography

Sharrin Rees Photography

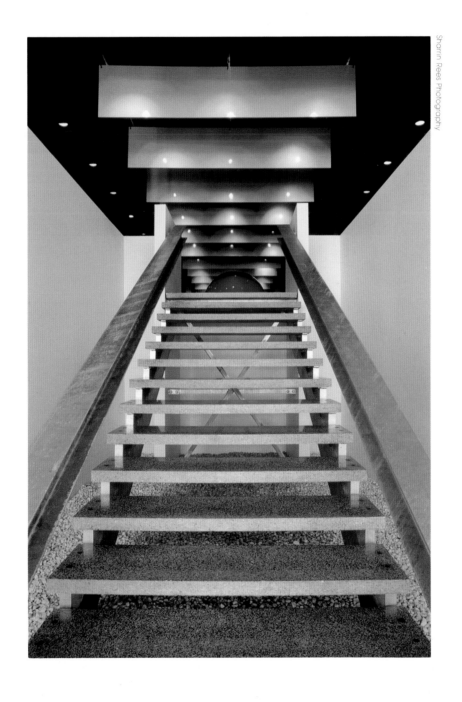

Sharrin Rees Photography

ISSEY MIYAKE WOMEN

PRODUCT: Women's clothing
London, England

Stanton · Williams' basic task for Issey Miyake Women was to transform a small ground floor retail space with a separate lower office and stock area into a unified retail environment.

The designers created a scheme which clearly links the new lower retail space to the street level by the removal of most of the ground floor to create a grand double-height stairwell volume. This link is emphasized by the visual connection of a single linear ceiling coffer and skylight to a 22-foot-high translucent window at the end of the space, thus concentrating the movement down to the lower area.

The use of natural materials in the lower space, such as oiled and whitened oak, raw silk and canvas, a pale gray granolithic floor, limestone pavers, raw concrete and sealed white plaster walls, contribute tactile and feminine qualities to the Zen-like space.

Responding to Issey Miyake's strong forms and subtle fabrics, Stanton · Williams created a simple yet flexible studio-type space that would allow for freedom of movement and change to occur—qualities inherent in Miyake's clothing.

CLIENT: **Issey Miyake Women** PRODUCT: **Women's clothing** DESIGN FIRM: **Stanton · Williams** PRINCIPALS IN CHARGE: **Alan Stanton and Paul Williams** DESIGN TEAM: **Robert Letts, Alan Farlie, Kulbir Chadha, Michael Langley** PHOTOGRAPHY: **Peter Cook**

Peter Cook

MOSS SHOWROOM

PRODUCT: Clothing
New York, NY

Faced with a complex program which required integration of a showroom and residence for a New York based fashion designer, the architects set out with a rigorous proposal based on redefining and configuring the building's structure and envelope. Casual beam and girder placements were adjusted to align and "idealize" the space.

In addition to the rehabilitation of the existing space, new elements were added: living-dining rooms, kitchen, bedroom and bath were created, as well as the addition of a show area.

At the entrance, an over-scaled pair of sliding and pivoting steel doors offer closure, direction and a sense of movement. The steel ring inscribed into the floor traces and notates the arc of the door "swings."

Bleached maple flooring, wall paneling and cabinetry have been used throughout tending to soften any austere connotations which might be perceived from an architecture so well versed in the modernist language.

CLIENT: **Murray Moss** PRODUCT: **Clothing** ARCHITECTS: **Smith-Miller + Hawkinson**
PARTNER IN CHARGE: **Henry Smith-Miller** PHOTOGRAPHY: © **Matteo Piazza;**
© **Paul Warchol**

© Matteo Piazza

URBANE USA/PHOTONICA

PRODUCT: Image bank and photo studio
New York, NY

Urbane USA and Photonica's program required that two separate and independent operations utilizing a common reception area and conference room be housed adjacent to one another. The image bank required a quiet, dust-free environment accessible to the public. The photo studio, on the other hand, is a busy and highly trafficked space with a private function. Chatham's design solution was based on constructing two parallel walls which run the entire width of the space and accommodate various storage recesses, in addition to providing thick insulated sound breaks between the reception studio and image bank.

An iconic element is provided at the entrance to the image bank—an over-scaled, splayed yellow plywood door, reminiscent of an actual bank vault, is counterpoised by a green sliding door to the photo studio.

The remaining elements and fixtures throughout the space, such as the maple plywood reception desk and the elegant rolling work tables, have been kept utilitarian and are constructed from common materials.

CLIENT: **Urbane USA and Photonica**   PRODUCT: **Image bank and photo studio**
ARCHITECT: **Walter Chatham**   FURNITURE: **Jonas Milder**   PHOTOGRAPHY:
© **Michael Moran**

© Michael Moran Inset © Michael Moran

ART TO USE

PRODUCT: Art-furniture
Frankfurt, Germany

Ulrike Muller's Art To Use design gallery is located in the heart of Frankfurt, in the courtyard of a building dating from the early German Empire. The gallery's usable area is spread over two floors, a mezzanine and a basement.

Owing to the low ceiling heights, both the client and the architect decided to open the floor slab next to the central slab so that a more unified view of the spaces would be possible. An atrium-like space is therefore established in the center, affording glimpses of almost all parts of the gallery. The transparency of this central zone is accentuated by a metal net, which suits the existing architectural atmosphere.

Demolished areas were notated on the existing asphalt floor, which, due to its industrial nature, was left intact. Wherever possible, existing features like radiators and steel columns were stripped to their original colors and waxed. Car headlamps were used as lighting throughout due to their streamlined form and utilitarian character.

Art To Use exhibits some of the more well-known European furniture designers and artists, such as Borek Sipek, Ron Arad, Andre Dubreuil, Danny Lane and others.

Felix Borkenau, Hamburg

CLIENT: **Art To Use**   PRODUCT: **Art-furniture**   ARCHITECT: **Volker Albus**
PHOTOGRAPHY: **Jeanette Schaun; Felix Borkenau, Hamburg**

Jeanette Schaun, Hamburg

Jeanette Schaun, Hamburg

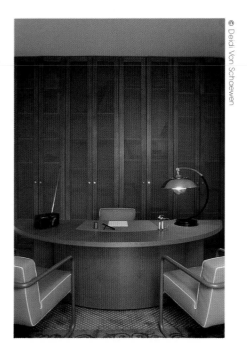

ECART
PRODUCT: Contemporary furniture *Paris, France*

Andrée Putman established Ecart to produce distinctive furniture that she considers to be among the most exemplary creations of the twentieth century.

Converted from a former warehouse on rue Saint Antoine, the Ecart showroom harbors traces from its previous function, as seen in its extraordinary glass roof and industrial caged lift. The interior spaces have been restructured and the staircase redesigned.

The objects shown on these pages—furniture by Mariano Fortuny, Paul Mathieu & Michael Ray; mirror by Eileen Gray; aquarium by American theater director Robert Wilson—reflect Ms. Putman's philosophy based on simplicity and timelessness.

CLIENT: **Andrée Putman** PRODUCT: **Contemporary furniture** DESIGN FIRM: **Ecart** DESIGNER: **Andrée Putman** PHOTOGRAPHY: **Deidi Von Schaewen, Roland Beaufre**

FONTANA ARTE
PRODUCT: Lighting
Los Angeles, CA

The new Fontana Arte showroom at DIVA, a high-profile design store on Beverly Boulevard in Los Angeles, represents the first showroom/retail store in the United States by this well-honored Italian lighting manufacturer. Veteran Italian architects Franco Raggi and Daniela Puppa were called upon to help establish the company's new American presence.

Confronted with a rectangular space of 200 square meters and a glass facade, the architects conceived of a space based upon weightlessness and flexibility. They created three movable partitions with large openings/passages. These suspended walls are fixed to the ceiling by delicate white tubes that run parallel, rotated to the street front. Conceptually they lend a theatrical character to the space, allowing the lighting-objects to reverberate amidst the physicality of the architecture. The walls are finished in a sanded texture and two sponged colors, gray for the movable walls and brick red for the perimeter, evoking a rough Mediterranean "intonaco." The floor pavement was created by mixing a thin layer of resin with gray concrete.

At the entrance, a free-standing "architectural quotation" refers to the original "real" arch at the first Fontana Arte showroom located in an old Milanese palace in via Montenapolene 3. This arch works as a permanent signifier and can be found at all Fontana Arte stands and showrooms in Italy and abroad.

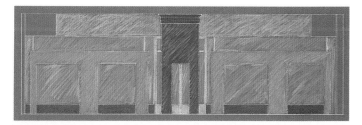

CLIENT: **Fontana Arte** PRODUCT: **Lighting** DESIGN FIRM: **Franco Raggi and Daniela Puppa Architects** COLLABORATOR: **Mario Falci** PHOTOGRAPHY: **Grey Crawford**

Grey Crawford

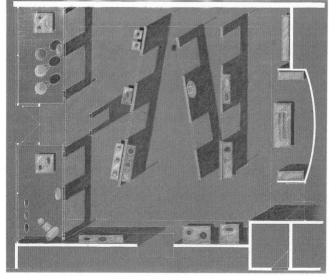

PALAZZO REIMER
PRODUCT: Contemporary furniture
Venice, Italy

The Italian architect Paolo Piva was called in for the renovation of Palazzo Reimer on the Grand Canal in Venice—an inherently beautiful location. The light-filled showroom displays some of Italy's more established furniture companies.

Producing a restoration with loving care is second nature for a truly Italian designer of Piva's stature. All doors, windows, ceilings and floors have been carefully restored and refinished. An ancient Venetian stucco technique for walls has been used in abundance, projecting a warm sensuality that runs throughout the project.

In totality, Palazzo Reimer provides a strikingly beautiful setting for contemporary Italian furniture design, understated in its elegance.

CLIENT: **Palazzo Reimer** PRODUCT: **Contemporary furniture** DESIGNER:
Paolo Piva, Architect PHOTOGRAPHY: **Jean-François Jaussand**

Jean-François Jaussand

Jean-François Jaussand

Jean-François Jaussand

Jean-François Jaussand

Jean-François Jaussand

Jean-François Jaussand

Jean-François Jaussand

Jean-François Jaussand

Jean-François Jaussand

Jean-François Jaussand

Jean-François Jaussand

Jean-François Jaussand

Jean-François Jaussand

Jean-François Jaussand

Jean-François Jaussand

Jean-François Jaussand

ec · cen · tric *adj* individualistic, narrative, idiosyncratic and mannerist.

ONE OFF LTD.
PRODUCT: Contemporary furniture
London, England

Ron Arad's new digs for One Off Ltd. and his own architectural and design studio are located far from the "maddening" crowd, nestled away from curiosity seekers. A flying, winged volume of space soars amid crumbling buildings, in an old ramshackle courtyard, on Chalk Farm Road, in northwest London.

Internationally known for his furniture endeavors, Arad here has erected an expressive piece of emotive architecture, striking in its conception and execution. Its sensual, tensioned roof membrane is fabricated from expanded metal, PVC tensioned fabric, and steel. It derives its form from the curvature and compressive forces of its expanded metal shell. This is the first time "Expamet" has been used for a shell structure, and, as a result, load bearing tests were carried out by the City University in London to determine its buckling capacities.

Ron Arad and his design team experimented with every new element of the scheme, incorporating provocative ideas into the interior. The floor was conceived of as a lanscape allowing a transition between the showroom and design office without having to build a wall. The resulting "hill" accommodates a storage space for the air handling unit, which provides heat and air-conditioning through the display/bridge that vaults from the "hill" to the mezzanine offices.

CLIENT: **One Off Ltd.** PRODUCT: **Contemporary furniture** DESIGN FIRM: **Ron Arad Associates, Ltd.** PRINCIPAL IN CHARGE: **Ron Arad** PROJECT DESIGNERS: **Ron Arad and Alison Brooks, with Alex Meitlis** DESIGN TEAM: **Ron Arad, Alison Brooks, Caroline Thorman, Shaun Crown, Rachel Reynolds, Ian Whittaker, Matthew Stanwix, Jules Goss, Duncan McVean, Jacinta Lynch, Charles Walker, Monique van Den Hurk, Vincent Chang** PHOTOGRAPHY: **Christof Kircherer**

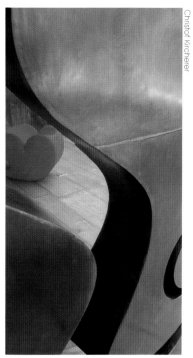

Christof Kircherer

Christof Kircherer

AZZEDINE ALAIA

PRODUCT: Women's clothing
New York, NY

Although he is not yet as well known for his decorating skills as for his accomplishments as an artist, painter/sculptor Julian Schnabel has created an artist's atelier for the fashion designer Azzedine Alaia, in Manhattan's always fashionable SoHo district.

With the usual pomp and circumstance for which he is infamous in the art world, Schnabel has here applied his talents to a more commercial endeavor. Approaching his task with characteristic bravado, he used 10-inch-wide construction planks for the floors and created "Giacomettiesque" bronze garment racks, counterpoised against lush wine-colored velvet drapery at the entrance to the fitting rooms. The retro-fitted Louis XIV display tables and reception desk sit uncomfortably amid the large Schnabel totems and fittings, but nicely serve to illustrate the "enfant terrible" decorating concepts employed within.

Jeff Vaughan

Peter Margonelli

CLIENT: **Azzedine Alaia** PRODUCT: **Women's clothing** DESIGNER: **Julian Schnabel** PHOTOGRAPHY: **Peter Margonelli, Jeff Vaughan**

Peter Margonelli

SPAZIO ROMEO GIGLI
PRODUCT: Men's and women's clothing
New York, NY

Housed in an Upper East Side Manhattan townhouse, "The Spazio," as it is referred to, represents Romeo Gigli's first showroom/retail operation in the United States. His initial impulse was to strip the existing shell down to its original structure and "resurrect the light."

The inherent design qualities reflect Gigli's baroque, yet utterly modern sensibility, as is evident in the artful and playful contrasts contained throughout the Spazio. Fanciful decorations, beaded glass work, and trompe-l'oeil drapery stand in direct juxtaposition to the exposed industrial air-conditioning, halogen strung lighting fixtures, and the minimal architectural container. The furniture is comprised strictly of twentieth-century Italian pieces by the likes of Mollino, De Carli, Munari and Fornasetti.

The American artist Kris Ruhs contributed the decorations in the floors, stairwells and elevator.

CLIENT: **Romeo Gigli** PRODUCT: **Men's and women's clothing** DESIGNER: **Romeo Gigli with Kris Ruhs** PHOTOGRAPHY: **Matteo Piazza**

SUCCHI FOOTWEAR

PRODUCT: Stylish footwear
Melbourne, Australia

Tom Kovac's organically inspired design for Succhi Footwear is the result of a hands-on approach to design. This project changed several times during the construction process. By continually checking building progress, Kovac decided to shelve his initial design for a vaulted ceiling in favor of a continuous wall/ceiling membrane. Also, a jarrah timber floor discovered during construction was left intact.

Succhi Footwear evokes the feeling of a primitive "womb-like cavern." Its white plaster interior reasserts the dramatic sculpted form and engages the merchandise. With a sweeping gesture, the graceful wall/ceiling structure seems to hover effortlessly in space. Pod-like slits carved into the vault serve as lighting coffers.

Kovac also designed the animated chaise-lounge which darts across the center of the store, its shapely form echoing the organic nature of the design.

CLIENT: **Succhi Footwear** PRODUCT: **Stylish footwear** DESIGNER: **Tom Kovac,**
assisted by Andres Straube PHOTOGRAPHY: © **Trevor Mein Photography**

© Trevor Mein Photography

JOE BOXER-GIRLFRIEND

PRODUCT: Women's clothing
New York, NY

In a 400-square-foot showroom for Joe Boxer-Girlfriend, Kennedy/Page Associates have outdone themselves with a project full of camp and wry humor.

Black and white with flourishes of gold abound. Custom quilted fabric walls with brass studs serve as the setting. Faux painted bas-relief mirror frames, poised against an entire wall framed in gilt, highlight the product display wall.

Of particular note are the suspended, 360-degree platinum blond "wig chandeliers" which gleefully hang over the black lacquer bio-morphic selling tables.

Here, a stripe becomes visual relief.

CLIENT: **Joe Boxer-Girlfriend** PRODUCT: **Women's clothing** DESIGN FIRM: **Kennedy/Page Associates, Inc.** PARTNERS IN CHARGE: **Patrick Kennedy and Peter Page** PHOTOGRAPHY: **Photo Studio TuTu**

ANGELO TARLAZZI

PRODUCT: Men's and women's clothing
New York, NY

In a double-height rectilinear volume of space on West 57th Street, aestheticians Paul Mathieu and Michael Ray have worked their charm.

The well-appointed grand salon of Angelo Tarlazzi's fashion empire recalls the decorative impulse which flourished from the pencils of men like Jacques-Emile Ruhlmann, Andre Arbus and Louis Sue, namely the great French Art Deco designers. However, history lessons aside, Mathieu and Ray's decorative talents lie in their keen ability to anticipate the direction of the fashion set. Here, images can acquire hidden meanings, and a newly purchased outfit can take on cherished significance. Regardless, the intelligence at work here is quite apparent.

Cream-colored walls and carpeting are counterpoised against rubbed oak pilasters and elegantly draped curtains that infuse the space with an undeniable glamour. On the mezzanine level, which overlooks the grand salon, red leather-upholstered dressing room doors are interspersed with luscious red drapes, further dramatizing the haute couture theatrics.

The designers are not without a sense of humor, as is evidenced by their custom furniture designs, Pompeii-inspired clothing carts, and neoclassical/modern side chairs from which Mr. Tarlazzi's monogram, the letter A, is suspended within a sylized T.

Jeff Vaughan

CLIENT: **Angelo Tarlazzi** PRODUCT: **Men's and women's clothing** DESIGNERS: **Paul Mathieu and Michael Ray** PHOTOGRAPHY: **Jeff Vaughan**

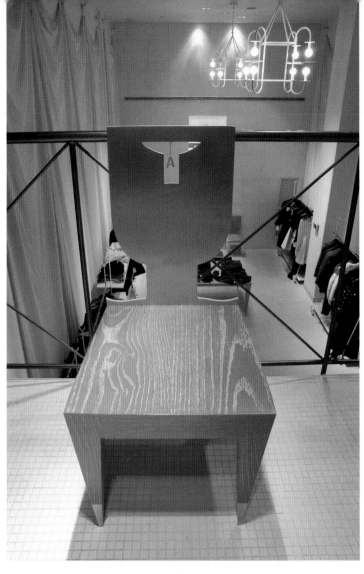

JIGSAW
PRODUCT: Clothing
Brompton Road, London, England

Nigel Coates and Doug Branson have continually applied an experimental attitude to design. Armed with their narrative concepts of architecture, their approach to a project is more akin to a film maker grooming a cinematic experience. Thus, design becomes a "theatre of signs" which materializes the territory of ideas, synthesizing the unexpected with the familiar. Their juxtaposition of a modern sense of movement and spatial qualities with the more traditional qualities inherent in an arts and craft sense of detailing, has led some critics to refer to their work as Industrial Baroque, for lack of a better term.

For the Jigsaw projects, such as the flagship shop shown here, Branson Coates' theories have evolved to yet a more symphonic level. The double-height glass facade, with its sensual, copper-clad column, allows a tantalizing glimpse into the main upper salon. The approach across the stone paved floor leads up the grand sweeping staircase, which is evocatively detailed and fabricated. A spectacular Coates-designed chandelier, from which blue glass pod-like shapes are suspended, awaits the customer at the top. At the perimeter of the room, the artist Stuart Helm was commissioned to paint a mural to reflect the sun-drenched colors of the clothing.

Other noteworthy details include Nigel Coates' upholstered "tongue" armchairs, huge hammered-metal mirrors that face each other across the center of the room, custom console tables, and mannequins. Coates' "spring" lamps from previous Jigsaw shops have been applied here to wall fittings as well as to a spiraling light track and recessed ceiling fixtures.

CLIENT: **Jigsaw Shop** PRODUCT: **Clothing** DESIGN FIRM: **Branson Coates Architecture** PARTNER IN CHARGE: **Nigel Coates** PROJECT ARCHITECT: **Gerrard O'Carrol** DESIGNER: **Dominic Tolson** PHOTOGRAPHY: © **1991 Chris Gascoigne/Arcaid**

J. MORGAN PUETT

PRODUCT: Women's clothing
New York, NY

J. Morgan Puett's space, set in a garage-like environment in downtown Manhattan, reveals some striking material juxtapositions rich in associative qualities.

Almost Amish- or Shaker-style clothing is displayed on rusted metal fittings in front of battered metal-clad walls. Dilapidated machine parts are casually placed around the space, as though the former shop steward ran out and forgot to return, or perhaps to remind us of a past now long forgotten.

Holes in the ceilings and walls have been covered with sheets of scrap metal that are nailed into place. Painted American wood furniture is propped up in the corners, and clothes, hanging from chains, line the front window.

Clearly paying no heed to well-worn merchandising credos, J. Morgan Puett has created a small, evocative and poetic shop, using what other, less-talented people simply would have thrown out, or even worse, covered up.

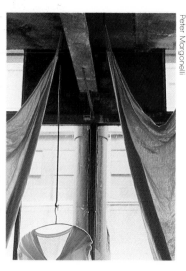

CLIENT: **J. Morgan Puett** PRODUCT: **Women's clothing** DESIGNER:
J. Morgan Puett PHOTOGRAPHY: **Peter Margonelli**

syn·thet·ic *adj* telematic, Pop culture, anti-nostalgia and hybrid.

BAROVIER & TOSO

PRODUCT: Lighting and objects in Murano glass
Milan, Italy

A nine-meter-long Venetian chandelier of outlandish and whimsical design is suspended within a cobalt blue volume of space on via Montenapoleone 1, in Milan. Murano glass chandeliers and lighting fixtures of various colors and shapes are housed in containers designed as little stages/exhibition niches, surrounded by golden frames. Light metal structures accommodate the display of smaller objects, such as vases, glasses, and other decorative items.

Franco Raggi has created a Pandora's box, architecturally divided in two parts. The lower (street) level lacks a ceiling and works primarily as a window. A narrow, diagonal gold staircase provides ascendance to the upper level which acts as an exhibition area balcony. The ceiling is painted gold.

The flooring has been treated with a mixture of epoxy blue resin and fine black marble dust.

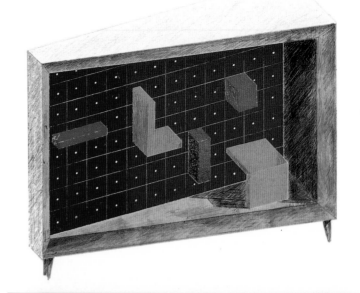

Miro Zagnoli Fotografo, Milan

CLIENT: **Barovier & Toso**   PRODUCT: **Lighting and objects in Murano glass**
DESIGNER: **Franco Raggi, Architect, with Mario Falci**   PHOTOGRAPHY:
Miro Zagnoli Fotografo, Milan

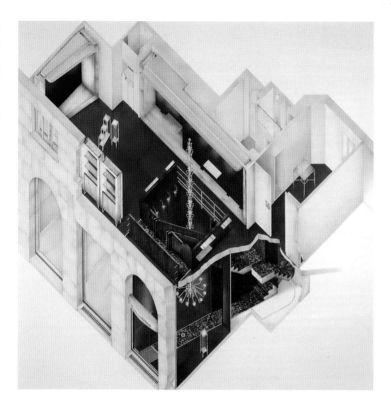

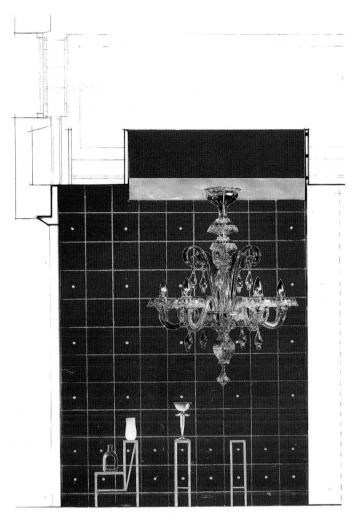

GLASSTATION OVA
PRODUCT: Glass, mirrors
Tokyo, Japan

In the Aoyama area in Tokyo, Shigeru Uchida has created a bold and synthetic environment for the display and understanding of glass, mirrors and related construction materials. Unlike the typical showroom, most of the samples are installed in the wall units in order to emphasize the overall integration of space. The freestanding, stripped, studded antico stucco and sandblasted glass walls created a highly graphic architectural envelope within the space.

Glasstation Ova not only functions as a showroom, but also as a gallery space, meeting room, small lecture hall and workshop for professionals and the general public to gather materials, information and knowledge on glass products and resources.

CLIENT: **Glasstation Ova** PRODUCT: **Glass, mirrors** DESIGN FIRM: **Studio 80**
DESIGNER: **Shigeru Uchida** PHOTOGRAPHY: © **Nacása & Partners**

MARCATRÉ

PRODUCT: Contract furniture
Madrid, Spain

On Calle de Claudio Coello in Madrid, Perry King and Santiago Miranda have designed a showroom for Marcatré, an Italian contract furniture company. Marcarté requested that both the showroom and offices be accommodated within the 12,000-square-foot space.

At the entrance, a curved wall constructed from painted timber panels clad in a fine bronze mesh serves as an arcade, suggesting direction and defining showroom areas. This bronze mesh wall pierces through several architectural facades as it cuts its way toward the rear of the showroom. The first element that it encounters is a bowed, almond-shaped gate with silk-screened stratified glass framed in stainless steel. The other, secondary (solid) element, counterpoised against this arcade, is a granite-clad orthogonal wall which denotes a special raised display pavilion within the showroom complex. The offices are housed in the arched entry "de Chiricoesque" volumes.

Various optical and spatial devices have been used, such as the recessed mirrors in niches which reflect the skewed dynamic volumes and enlarge the spaces. Lighting throughout was designed by King Miranda for Arteluce.

CLIENT: **Marcatré** PRODUCT: **Contract furniture** DESIGN FIRM: **King Miranda Associati** PARTNERS IN CHARGE: **Perry A. King and Santiago Miranda, with Malcolm S. Inglis** PHOTOGRAPHY: **Andrea Zani**

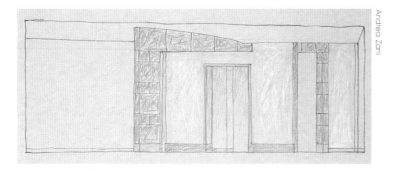

Andrea Zani

Andrea Zani

EDRA

PRODUCT: Upholstered furniture
Sardinia, Italy

For Edra, an Italian-based upholstered seating company, Massimo Morozzi has initiated a new series of marketing directives based on a theoretical narrative, which Edra conceives of as a fresher and more direct form of communication.

Morozzi's "Room Tales" sets seek to narrate cinematic stories or themes yet simultaneously speak on a level intrinsically removed from the relentless, cyclical nature of consumerism. Morozzi's "fake settings" are iconoclastic commentaries on the way we seek to view the world, and how we want others to view us. Here, Morozzi has snatched images borrowed from pop cliches, American kitsch, MTV culture, and old movies, not as models to follow, but as linguistic codes which must be transcended in order to create new languages appropriate for the digitalized twenty-first century. One is led to recall an old alchemical credo, "there is not redemption, without corruption."

CLIENT: **Edra S.P.A.** PRODUCT: **Upholstered furniture** DESIGN FIRM: **Massimo Morozzi & Partners** DESIGNER: **Massimo Morozzi** PHOTOGRAPHY: **Giacomo Giannini, assisted by Luigi Manca**

Giacomo Giannini

Giacomo Giannini

Giacomo Giannini

Giacomo Giannini

Giacomo Giannini

Giacomo Giannini

Giacomo Giannini

JAPAN GORE-TEX

PRODUCT: Textiles
Tokyo, Japan

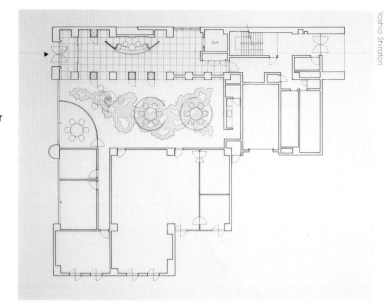

Corporate headquarters in Japan for the American company Gore-tex are located on the first floor of a new three-story office building in the Tokyo suburb of Setagaya. Well known as the manufacturer of Gore-tex, the company is now entering the field of comprehensive science. Masanori Umeda was chosen to design their Japan headquarters.

Umeda chose to extract scientific patterns from the inherent brief and use them in a decorative way. For example, magnified patterns of Gore-tex, as seen through an electron microscope, have been silk-screened onto the aluminum columns. Above the reception desk, fiber-optics were employed to indicate the Gore-tex global network.

In the main hall, Umeda referred to his own cultural tradition by expressing the idea of a *pao* (a Mongolian traditional house) such as those found on Mongolian plains. The room has an outdoor ambiance, with its cloud ceiling and circular partitions. These partitions are for display purposes and can have hangers and shelves fitted to them. Visual privacy is provided by using lightweight polycarbonate screens which can easily be moved if the space is being used for other occasions or exhibitions.

CLIENT: **Japan Gore-tex Inc.** PRODUCT: **Textiles** DESIGN FIRM: **U-MetaDesign, Inc.** DESIGNER: **Masanori Umeda** PHOTOGRAPHY: **Yoshio Shiratori**

MARCATRÉ
PRODUCT: Contract furniture
Bologna, Italy

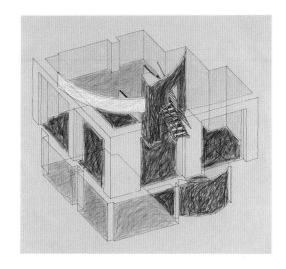

Marcatré is a contract furniture company with a well-established reputation in European markets. King Miranda has developed a long-standing relationship with Marcatré, designing several of their showrooms in various countries over the past ten years.

For their Bologna showroom, Marcatré requested a project of high visibility, reflecting confidence and optimism. Bologna is the center of the office furniture industry, and hence the hometown of some of its important competitors. The site Marcatré chose was a small cube-shaped space with two sides of glass frontage.

The designers wisely chose to divide the cubic space into two, both vertically and horizontally, as well as utilize the basement and also construct a mezzanine level for the staff. The insertion of a new staircase dynamically engages all three levels. The vertical division, made with a high curved wall, cuts diagonally across the plane and horizontally through the cube. This horizontal plane is extended across the cube by the lights suspended from the ceiling.

Through the implementation of some very clear spatial ideas, King Miranda has composed a project artfully conceived and executed.

CLIENT: **Marcatré** PRODUCT: **Contract furniture** DESIGN FIRM: **King Miranda Associati** PARTNERS IN CHARGE: **Perry A. King and Santiago Miranda**, with **Carlos Moys and Mauro Merkini** PHOTOGRAPHY: **Andrea Zani**

Andrea Zani

Andrea Zani

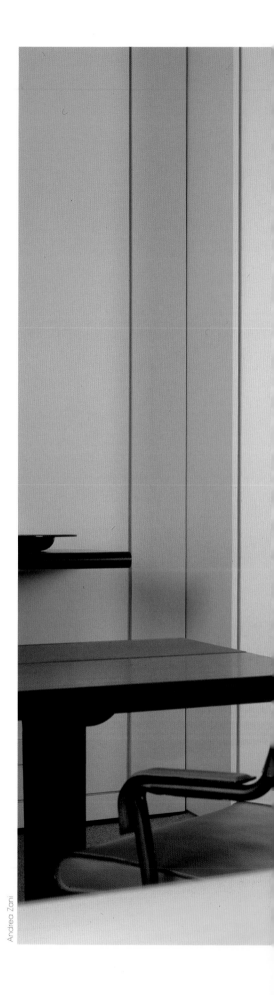

Andrea Zani

Andrea Zani

PHOTOGRAPHY **Studio Sai**

CLIENT: **Kinder Kind** PRODUCT: Children's clothing DESIGN FIRM: **Tsao and McKown Architects** PARTNERS IN CHARGE: Calvin Tsao and Zack McKown

Studio Sai

KINDER KIND II

PRODUCT: Children's clothing

Hong Kong

In their second Kinder Kind shop, Tsao and McKown have created an environment as envisioned through the eyes of a child. A child's reality is both imaginative and curious. The architects have responded to this by incorporating gestures of fantasy and whimsy, all fused within geometrical and scholarly references. The central conceptual narrative is composed of two rooms, or a "diptych of day and night." The first room evokes night and is composed of a circular domed ceiling, its interior painted to convey the infinite night sky, with white stars encircling a moon-shaped light fixture.

Scale is a recurring theme throughout as evidenced by the toy airplane suspended in flight, the oversized picture frame and the placement height of the objects. The clothes are sparingly on view, displayed on a mannequin perched on a metal rod or hung from a quilted wall-piece. The "night" room expresses theater and playfulness, with the cashier occupying a Punch and Judy stage set backed by a frozen wooden curtain.

The second room expresses "daytime" through the use of bright cheerful colors, a circular patch of grass in the floor, and flower pots on a shelf that displays shoes and gloves rather than real flowers. The ceiling breaks to reveal the brightly lit sky, where a mysterious black trap door suggests a hidden infinity beyond. Illuminated boxes inscribed in niches create "little worlds" to captivate the child's imagination. In a tongue-in-cheek gesture to the antiquities arrayed in Sir John Soane's London house, Kinder Kind displays clothing hung from a series of beams topped with wooden "metaphysical" heads.

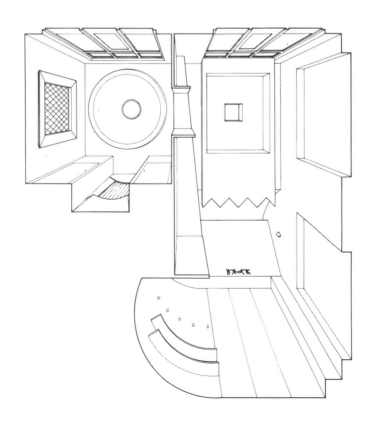

UNITED CHAIR

PRODUCT: Contract furniture
Washington, D.C.

For United Chair, Tom Gass has designed a metaphorical and disciplined graphic showroom, abstractly based on the American flag—an appropriate icon considering the showroom's location, in the nation's capital.

Curved walls, reception desk and vertical stars and stripes are white on white to subtly reinforce the overall concept and floor pattern. The cobalt blue ceiling adds life to the space. Various spatial exercises, like the mirror and sloped platform at the entrance, create a moving flag imagery; a half star butting into the mirror becomes whole, while the curved wall and product symmetrically complete the entrance area.

At the rear of the showroom, the carpet stripes curve up a rolled platform and the mirror continues on down into infinity. Stacking chairs are on a hidden dolly in the carpet, and the chairs are fixed at the top, thereby giving the illusion of weightlessness.

Overall, Tom Gass has contributed a new twist on "Old Glory," in a showroom full of heightened allusions and playful metaphors, in a spirit pure to its concept and execution.

CLIENT: **United Chair**   PRODUCT: **Contract furniture**   DESIGN FIRM: **Gass Design**
PRINCIPAL IN CHARGE: **Tom Gass**   PHOTOGRAPHY: **© Peter Paige**

© Peter Paige

© Peter Paige

© Peter Paige

© Peter Paige

cor·po·rate *adj* establishes, reflects corporate image/identity; transitional, classical.

KNOLL

PRODUCT: Contract and residential furniture
Frankfurt, Germany

The Frankfurt Knoll showroom space uses natural and primary shapes of classical furniture design: wood, metal, glass, circle, square and curve. Entry into the showroom, which doubles as an exhibition space, is via a white monochromatic gallery of stone and plaster terminated by a red reception desk. Major offices and a smaller conference room are formed by a series of parallel layered metal and glass screens threaded on an armature of converging steel beams. Designed as a counterpoint to complete privacy, the semi-transparent walls of perforated steel and glass maintain visual continuity of the showroom as a total display area, while also defining public and private zones.

The dominant design element of the showroom is a braced colonnade of thick rough-hewn spruce timber posts which forms a backdrop to the showroom, and which also serves to screen the offices and additional support spaces. The natural and unfinished wood stands as a metaphor for the symbolic root or essence of furniture, expressing the prima materia of furniture design and evoking the image of Laugier's "primitive hut."

CLIENT: **The Knoll Group** PRODUCT: **Contract and residential furniture**
ARCHITECT: **STUDIOS Architecture** PRINCIPAL: **Erik Sueberkrop** DESIGNERS: **Peter Van Dine and Arthur Collin with Max Durney** PHOTOGRAPHY: **Engelhardt & Sellin, Munich/courtesy of STUDIOS Architecture and The Knoll Group**

Engelhardt & Sellin, Munich

Engelhardt & Sellin, Munich

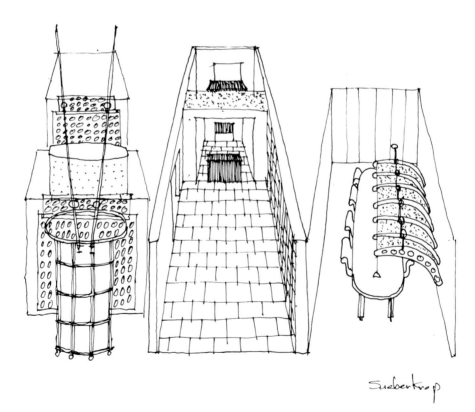

Sieberknop

Engelhardt & Sellin, Munich

CORNING

PRODUCT: Glass
New York, NY

In the 1850s Corning Glass Works moved to Corning, New York, to manufacture red and green glass lenses for railroad signal lights. A century and a half later, the altered transmission of light is a major component of Corning's business. Fiber optics, the next century's communication medium, is a product Corning helped invent and will continue to develop in the future.

Donovan and Green were asked to develop an entry to Corning's new international corporate headquarters in New York City. Extensive research led them to propose that the properties of glass and light, consistent elements the company has explored and been involved with, would make an appropriate vehicle to project the company's high-tech agenda.

Using dichroic filters, prisms, and optical mirrors combined with pure white point source lighting, a changing pattern of spectral light was focused on 50 feet of wall. Dichroic filters separate light into the various colors of the visible spectrum. By carefully selecting dichroic filters and aiming them through mirrors and prisms, the color palette becomes an ever-changing array. Light sources were programmed by computer so that the visual presentation constantly changes over the course of the day.

Utilizing basic optical principles of science and state-of-the-art technology, Donovan and Green's solution to explain Corning's technological advances communicates the essential aspects of Corning's corporate values, wrapped in a visual and educational experience.

© Wolfgang Hoyt Inset: © Wolfgang Hoyt

CLIENT: **Corning Corporate Headquarters**   PRODUCT: **Glass**   DESIGN FIRM: **Donovan and Green**   PARTNER IN CHARGE: **Michael Donovan**   DESIGNER: **Allen Wilpon**   PHOTOGRAPHY: © **Wolfgang Hoyt**

CORNING

Corning Incorporated
Steuben Offices

BENEDETTI
PRODUCT: Contract furniture
Los Angeles, CA

For Benedetti's Los Angeles showroom, Donovan and Green designed an arcade-like series of rooms constructed from exposed metal studs and metal mesh screening. When the screen/walls are lit, they produce a translucent, silvery gray moire effect. Displayed furniture can be lit from behind or in front of the metal scrim for a variety of visual effects.

Through the use of exposed construction materials, an interesting, lively dialogue takes place, which quietly contrasts with the more traditional contract-type furniture.

CLIENT: **Benedetti** PRODUCT: **Contract furniture** DESIGN FIRM: **Donovan and Green** PARTNER IN CHARGE: **Michael Donovan** DESIGN TEAM: **Kathy Saito, Patrick Noland, Allen Wilpon** PHOTOGRAPHY: **Roland Bishop Photography**

LEE BRAND ROOM

PRODUCT: Men's and women's clothing
Merriam, KS

The Lee Brand Room was developed in 5,000 square feet at the Lee corporate headquarters, to be used as a laboratory space.

Fitch RichardsonSmith's design incorporates the basics of American rural fixtures—barns, silos, train stations, covered wagons. The trusses that create the ceiling "wagon wheel" hold light tracks that spotlight different elements in the space. These structures, once part of the basic thread of the country, now convey honesty, quality and natural elements, all part of the Lee Company's outlook.

The architecture of the showroom is contemporary, yet established, representing the Lee Company's feeling of classic and casual. Tertiary colors are used to emphasize the natural elements and enhance the products displayed. The floors are covered in natural woven mat.

Photographic images underscore the company's credo of fit and comfort, which crosses age, gender and lifestyle. The showroom reflects Lee's identity and organizes products in a casual, yet effective manner.

CLIENT: **The Lee Company** PRODUCT: **Men's and women's clothing** DESIGN FIRM: **Fitch RichardsonSmith** DESIGNERS: **P. Kelly Mooney, Paul Lechleiter, Paul Westrick** ARCHITECTS: **Ellerbe Becket, Frank L. Schicchitano** PHOTOGRAPHY: **Mark A. Steele/Fitch Inc.**

Mark A. Steele/Fitch Inc.

Mark A. Steele/Fitch Inc.

Mark A. Steele/Fitch Inc.

Mark A. Steele/Fitch Inc.

Mark A. Steele/Fitch Inc.

Mark A. Steele/Fitch Inc.

KLEIN TOOLS

PRODUCT: Hand tools
Chicago, IL

The San Francsico Office of Gensler and Associates faced the design challenge of creating a memorable space in an old factory building for Klein Tools, a fifth-generation American business.

The new plan breaks up the conventional roofline over the renovated area and raises it to resemble the traditional two-tiered roof over forges and assembly lines. Two main areas under the modified roof provide a long rectangular boardroom and a small museum whose restricted light is appropriate for the display of the company's memorabilia and tools in a series of specially lighted jewel cases. The integral use of raw steel, stained gun-metal blue to portray a sense of depth, softened with wood accents and black asphalt tile floor further supports the industrial aesthetic.

Marco Lorenzetti/Hedrich Blessing

CLIENT: **Klein Tools, Inc.** PRODUCT: **Hand tools** DESIGN FIRM: **Gensler and Associates/Architects** PROJECT MANAGER: **Scott Kaufman** PROJECT DESIGNER: **James Wigglesworth** PHOTOGRAPHY: **Marco Lorenzetti/Hedrich Blessing**

CACHAREL
PRODUCT: Clothing
Paris, France

This prototype, designed by Sir Norman Foster and Partners for Cacharel clothing, is based on a modular concept that can be adapted for various commercial applications. Designs and packages for integration into existing buildings, shopping arcades (malls) and department store corners, were all thoughtfully considered according to Foster specifications.

CLIENT: **Cacharel** PRODUCT: **Clothing** DESIGN FIRM: **Sir Norman Foster and Partners** ARCHITECTS: **Sir Norman Foster and Partners** PHOTOGRAPHY: **Dennis Gilbert**

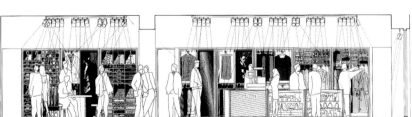

KNOLL

PRODUCT: Contract and residential furniture
Los Angeles, CA

Inspired by the indigenous architecture of the Hollywood Strip, Erica Pritchard divided the Knoll showroom space with seven pivoting "billboard" structures. Each billboard rotates a full 360 degrees, stands 8 feet high and 10 feet across, and displays enlarged design sketches from the hands of the Knoll masters.

With the feature of movable partitions in the form of rescreenable "billboards," the space can be redivided and restructured into various combinations, thus providing new conferencing zones, shared work areas, and displays.

Varying architectural devices were deployed in an effort to transcend the 11,000 square feet of warehouse expanse. A variety of floor levels, inexpensive yet rich materials, and skewed partition orientations were used to enhance the customers' procession through the various product vignettes. This new showroom provides an unusually flexible arena in which The Knoll Group may evolve its marketing and display strategies.

© Robert Kato Photography

CLIENT: **The Knoll Group** PRODUCT: **Contract and residential furniture**
DESIGNER: **Erica Pritchard** PROJECT MANAGER: **Karen Stone** PHOTOGRAPHY:
© **Robert Kato Photography**

HAGGAR GALLERY SOFTWEAR

PRODUCT: Men's clothing
New York, NY

Haggar, known for their more mature and professional men's apparel, decided to move into a younger, more casual market. Fitch RichardsonSmith was chosen to do the showroom renovation which was designed and installed in a remarkable six weeks.

The Gallery Softwear line had to be presented with an image that enhanced a slimmer, more youthful silhouette. Forms were designed to suggest both an athletic and casual influence. Advertising, merchandising and display techniques were integrated to give retailers potential applications to use in their stores.

Because the showroom was situated on the 31st floor of a downtown building, attention needed to be focused on the products and diverted from the views of the city beyond. The designers accomplished this by dropping Plexiglas panels in front of the windows with a description of the products surface-applied on the panels, as the most key features of the line are prominent in a bold accent color.

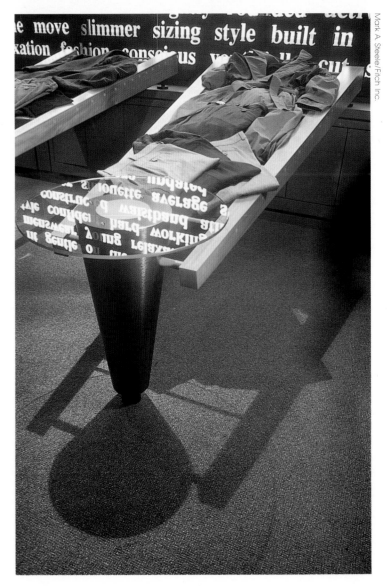

CLIENT: **Haggar Gallery Softwear** PRODUCT: **Men's clothing** DESIGN FIRM: **Fitch RichardsonSmith** PROJECT MANAGER/DESIGNER: **P. Kelly Mooney** DESIGNER: **Matthew Hern** MERCHANDISING CONSULTANT: **Beth Dorsey** PHOTOGRAPHY: **Mark A. Steele/Fitch Inc.**

Mark A. Steele/Fitch Inc.

ANDREW FEZZA
PRODUCT: Women's and men's clothing
New York, NY

Andrew Fezza's new fashion showroom, designed by Vicente Wolf Associates, totals some 4,000 square feet of space for reception, showroom, sales and offices.

Clearly defined selling zones of linen drapery run throughout the main selling floor, facilitating intimate spaces. For the private offices, which run along the perimeter walls, sisal carpeting, ancient artifacts, photographs and drawings add an affluent touch.

Materials and finishes which have become the hallmarks of Mr. Wolf's sensibility—pickled and limed oak flooring and fixtures, a mixture of traditional and custom-designed furniture, white and colored plaster walls—combine to create an eclectic and stylish setting for Mr. Fezza's young, "in the know" clientele.

Peter Vitale

CLIENT: **Andrew Fezza Company**   PRODUCT: **Women's and men's clothing**
DESIGN FIRM: **Vicente Wolf Associates**   PRINCIPAL IN CHARGE: **Vicente Wolf**
PHOTOGRAPHY: **Peter Vitale**

CHRISTOPHER HANSEN LTD.

PRODUCT: Audio/Video equipment
Beverly Hills, CA

New architectural elements were integrated into the restored exterior of a gracious late art-deco (c. 1940) building in Beverly Hills. Simple, clean materials—birch wood, black granite, clear and translucent glass—update the building's original exterior and reflect the high-tech merchandise within.

The 5,200-square-foot program required four acoustically engineered sound rooms for the display and operation of specialty audio equipment, a "THX-Dolby" video theater, a gallery hall with open space for flexibility, a video display room, a conference room and an employee lounge.

One enters through a small, copper-leafed rotunda which articulates and anchors the transition from the gallery to the hall that leads to the theater and displays futuristic jewelry, small appliances and accessories.

Period pieces in the main gallery, reminiscent of a potential client's home, provide a counterpoint to the plaster walls, black granite floors and birch wood, resulting in an elegant eclecticism.

CLIENT: **Christopher Hansen Ltd.** PRODUCT: **Audio/Video equipment** DESIGN FIRM: **Kirkpatrick Associates Architects, AIA** PROJECT DESIGNERS: **Grant C. Kirkpatrick and Stephen B. Straughan** PROJECT ARCHITECT: **Russell Hatfield** PROJECT ASSISTANTS: **Rachel Dougan, Cindy Utterback** PHOTOGRAPHY: **Weldon Brewster/Brewster & Brewster**

1   Entry
2   Gallery/Sales
3   Conference
4   Video Display
5   Listening Room
6   Toilet
7   Vestibule
8   Rotunda Display
9   Employee room
10 THX Theater
11 Corridor

FLOOR PLAN

Weldon Brewster/Brewster & Brewster

Weldon Brewster/Brewster & Brewster

APPENDIX

DESIGN FIRMS

Allies and Morrison Architects
54 Newman Street
London W1P 3PG
England

Anderson/Schwartz Architects
40 Hudson Street
New York, New York 10013

Axis Mundi
361 West 36th Street
New York, NY 10018

Branson Coates Architecture Limited
23 Old Street
London ECIV 9H0
England

Burley Katon Halliday
6A Liverpool Street
Paddington, N.S.W.
2021 Australia

Chatham, Walter
225 Lafayette Street
New York, New York 10012

Christopher Connell Design
570 Chapel Street
South Yarra, Melbourne, VIC 3141
Australia

Progetti Cordero
C.P. Company Sportswear, Inc.
680 Fifth Avenue, 25th Floor
New York, New York 10019

Din Associates Ltd.
6 South Lameth Place
London SW8 1SP
England

Donna Selene Seftel Architects
21 East 22nd Street, #3J
New York, New York 10010

Donovan and Green
333 7th Avenue
New York, New York 10001

Ecart s.a.
111 rue St. Antoine
75003 Paris
France

Edra S.P.a.
Divani E. Poltrone
Via Toscana 11
56030 Perignano, Pisa
Italy

Ellerbe Becket
605 West 47th Street, Suite 200
Kansas City, Missouri 64112

Fitch RichardsonSmith
10350 Olentangy River Road
P.O. Box 360
Worthington, Ohio 43085

Franco Raggi, Daniela Puppa Architects
Vicolo Calusca 10
20123 Milan
Italy

Gass Design
228 Warren Street
Brooklyn, New York 11201

Gensler and Associates/Architects
550 Kearney Street
San Francisco, California 94108

Gigli, Romeo
21 East 69th Street, 5th Floor
New York, New York 10021

J. Morgan Puett, Inc.
527 Broome Street
New York, New York 10013

Kennedy/Page Associates, Inc.
2421 Lake Pancoast Drive
Miami Beach, Florida 33190

King-Miranda Associati
Via Forcella 3
20144 Milan
Italy

Kirkpatrick Associates Architects, AIA
1081 National Boulevard, Suite 104
Los Angeles, California 90064

KOVAC
19-25 Windsor Place
Melbourne, VIC 3000
Australia

Mathieu & Ray
12 rue Matheron
13100 Aix en Provence
France

Morphosis
2041 Colorado Avenue
Santa Monica, California 90404

Paolo Piva, Architect
San Paolo 2765B
3100 Venice
Italy

Powell-Tuck Associates, Ltd.
12 Barley Mow Passage
London W4 4PH
England

Ron Arad Associates, Ltd.
62 Chalk Farm Road
London NWI 8AN
England

Sir Norman Foster and Partners
Riverside Three
22 Hester Road
London SW11 4AN
England

Smith-Miller + Hawkinson, Architects
305 Canal Street
New York, New York 10013

Stanton • Williams
10 Huguenot Place
Heneage Street
London E1 5LJ
England

Studio 80
1-17-14 Minami-Aoyama
Minato-ku
Tokyo 107
Japan

Studio Citterio/Dwan
Via Lovanio, 8
20121 Milan
Italy

STUDIOS Architecture
99 Green Street
San Francisco, California 94111

Tsao & Mckown Arch.
41 East 42nd Street
New York, New York 10017

Umberto Riva, Architect
c/o Umbrella SRL
Viole Felissent, 48
31100 Treviso
Italy

U-MetaDesign, Inc.
1-8-3 Nishiazabu
Minato-ku
Tokyo 106
Japan

Uvegi Associates, Inc.
210 West 70th Street
New York, New York 10023

Vicente Wolf Associates
333 West 39th Street
New York, New York 10018

Zweig, Peter
8114 Meadow Crest Drive
Houston, Texas 77071

PHOTOGRAPHERS

Assassi, Farshid
Assassi Productions
P.O. Box 3651
Santa Barbara, California 93139

Basilico, Gabriele
Piazza Tricolore, 4
Milano
Italy

Beaufre, Roland
Agency Top
15 rue de Verneuil
Paris 75007
France

Borkenau, Felix
Moorfuhrtweg #9
2000 Hamburg 60
Germany

Brewster, Weldon
Brewster & Brewster Photography
429 1/2 West California Avenue
Glendale, California 91203

Cook, Peter
300 Saint John Street
London EC1U4PP
England

Crawford, Grey
1714 Lyndon Street
South Pasadena, California 91030

Engelhardt & Sellin, Munich
G-Daimler-Strasse 35
7141 Murr
Germany

Galatis, Michael
1302 Cedar Hill Avenue
Dallas, Texas 15208

Gascoigne, Chris
c/o Marysia Woronieka Publicity
208 Fulham Road
London
England

Giannini, Giacomo
Corso C. Colombo 4
20144 Milan
Italy

Gilbert, Dennis
c/o Sir Norman Foster and Partners
Riverside Three
22 Hester Road
London SW114AN
England

Hueber, Eduard
Arch Photo
104 Sullivan Street
New York, New York 10012

Jaussand, Jean-François
7 rue de l'Abbe Grouit
75015 Paris
France

John Edward Linden Photography
113 Wymering Mansions, Wymering Road
Maida Vale
London W92NF
England

Kircherer, Christof
c/o Ron Arad Associates
62 Chalk Farm Road
London NWI8AN
England

Licata, Jeffrey
4618 Beach 46th Street
Brooklyn, New York 11224

Lorenzetti, Marco
Hedrich/Blessing Ltd.
11 West Illinois Street
Chicago, Illinois 60610

Margonelli, Peter
524 Broadway, 6th Floor
New York, New York 10013

Michael Moran Photography
245 Mulberry Street, #14
New York, New York 10012

Nacása & Partners inc.
3-5-5 Minami Azabu Minato-ku
Tokyo 106
Japan

Paige, Peter
269 Parkside Road
Harrington, New Jersey 07640

Paul Warchol Photography Inc.
133 Mulberry Street, #65
New York, New York 10013

Peterson, Jan
560 South Main Street
Los Angeles, California 90013

Photo Studio TuTu Ltd.
240 Central Park South
New York, New York 10019

Piazza, Matteo
Corso di Porta Ticinese 69
20123 Milan
Italy

Radino, Francesco
c/o Umbrella SRL
Viale Felissent, 48
31100 Treviso
Italy

Robert Kato Photography
529 West 42nd Street, #9V
New York, New York 10036

Roland Bishop Photography
30 North Raymond Avenue, #803
Pasadena, California 91103

Schaun, Jeanette
Oberhafenstoope 1
2000 Hamburg 1
Germany

Schierlitz, Tom
Schierlitz & Budewig Inc.
242 West 38th Street, PH
New York, New York 10018

Sharrin Rees Photography
6A Liverpool Street
Paddington, NSW 2021
Australia

Shiratori, Yoshio
#501 Odakyu Shinanomacki M/S
5-3 Minami Motomaki Shinjuku-ku
Tokyo
Japan

Steele, Mark A.
Fitch Inc.
10350 Olentangy River Road
P.O. Box 360
Worthington, Ohio 43085

Trevor Mein Photography
26 Vessi Street
Northcote, Victoria, 3070
Australia

Vaughan, Jeff
51 White Street, #52
New York, New York 10013

Vitale, Peter
P.O. Box 10128
Santa Fe, New Mexico 87504

Von Schaewen, Deidi
c/o Ecart s.a.
111 rue St. Antoine
75004 Paris
France

Wolfgang Hoyt Photography
18 West 27th Street
New York, New York 10001

Miro Zagnoli Fotografo
Alzaia Naviglio Grande 156
20144 Milan
Italy

Zani, Andrea
Via Crema 29
20435 Milan
Italy

INDEX

ARCHITECTURAL/DESIGN FIRMS

PHOTOGRAPHY

ACKNOWLEDGMENTS

I would like to sincerely thank the following individuals, who each in their own way have contributed significantly toward the making of this book. First, many thanks must go to Kevin Clark for suggesting and encouraging this project, Susan Kapsis for her insightful comments, Carrie Abel, and the entire PBC International staff for their diligent follow-throughs from my endless stream of faxes.

I am indebted to Marta Gale at *Interior Architecture* (Australia) for her familiarity with projects Down Under, Marcus Field at *Designers Journal* (London) and Mikato Oikawa at *W.IN.D.* (Tokyo) for their suggestions and contacts from their respective parts of the globe, as well as Margaret Janik, Harry Uvegi, Mitchell White, Jeff Licata, Stefania Zamparelli, Monique Abramoff, David Shaw Nicholls and all the many talented photographers whose work illustrates this book.

Finally, I would like to express my gratitude to Thom Mayne for his provocative foreword, Ross Anderson, Terry Dwan, Henry Smith-Miller, Shigeru Uchida and Masanori Umeda for their intelligent and personal essays. To all, my humble thanks.